MINECRAFT™

RANDOM HOUSE

WORLDS
NEW YORK

Stay safe online. Any website addresses listed in this book are correct at the time of going to print. However, Random House Worlds is not responsible for content hosted by third parties. Please be aware that online content can be subject to change and websites can contain content that is unsuitable for children. We advise that all children are supervised when using the Internet. This publisher does not have any control over and does not assume any responsibility for author or third-party websites or their content.

ONLINE SAFETY FOR YOUNGER FANS
Spending time online is great fun! Here are a few simple rules to help younger fans stay safe and keep the Internet a great place to spend time:
- Never give out your real name—don't use it as your username.
- Never give out any of your personal details.
- Never tell anybody which school you go to or how old you are.
- Never tell anybody your password except a parent or guardian.
- Be aware that you must be 13 or over to create an account on many sites. Always check the site policy and ask a parent or guardian for permission before registering.
- Always tell a parent or guardian if something is worrying you.

Random House Worlds
An imprint of Random House
A division of Penguin Random House LLC
1745 Broadway, New York, NY 10019
randomhousebooks.com
penguinrandomhouse.com

Copyright © 2025 by Mojang AB. All rights reserved.
Minecraft, the Minecraft logo, the Mojang Studios logo and the Creeper logo are trademarks of the Microsoft group of companies.

Penguin Random House values and supports copyright. Copyright fuels creativity, encourages diverse voices, promotes free speech, and creates a vibrant culture. Thank you for buying an authorized edition of this book and for complying with copyright laws by not reproducing, scanning, or distributing any part of it in any form without permission. You are supporting writers and allowing Penguin Random House to continue to publish books for every reader. Please note that no part of this book may be used or reproduced in any manner for the purpose of training artificial intelligence technologies or systems.

Random House is a registered trademark, and Random House Worlds and colophon are trademarks of Penguin Random House LLC.

Published in hardcover in the United Kingdom by Farshore, an imprint of HarperCollins Publishers Limited.

ISBN 978-0-593-98416-1
Ebook ISBN 978-0-593-98417-8

Printed in the United States on acid-free paper

2 4 6 8 9 7 5 3 1

First US Edition

Written by Tom Stone
Additional illustrations by George Lee
Special thanks to Sherin Kwan, Alex Wiltshire, Kelsey Ranallo, Lauren Marklund, Elin Roslund and Milo Bengtsson

Book Team: Production editor: Jocelyn Kiker • Managing editor: Susan Seeman
Production manager: Nathalie Mairena

The authorized representative in the EU for product safety and compliance is Penguin Random House Ireland, Morrison Chambers, 32 Nassau Street, Dublin D02 YH68, Ireland, https://eu-contact.penguin.ie.

MINECRAFT
MAGICAL
BITE-SIZE
BUILDS

WITH OVER 20 MARVELOUS MINI PROJECTS

CONTENTS

INTRODUCTION 5
GENERAL BUILD TIPS 6
MAGIC MIRROR 8
MERMAID LAGOON 10
GIANT BEANSTALK 14
MAGICIAN'S HAT. 20
FEROCIOUS DRAGON 22
BUBBLEGUM COTTAGE. 28
ENCHANTING TOWER 34
PUMPKIN CARRIAGE 38
ROYAL FROG 42
GLOWING MUSHROOM 44
HOUSE IN A SHOE 48
ALEBRIJE STATUES 52
BANANA-SPLIT BASE 56
FLOATING TEA PARTY 60
DRAGON ROLLER COASTER 64
SPELLBOOK SHOP 70
GENIE-LAMP BOAT 74
EMERALD APARTMENTS 76
FAIRY-TALE PALACE 82
ATLANTIS ABODE 88
COMBINATION CHALLENGES 92
GOODBYE 94

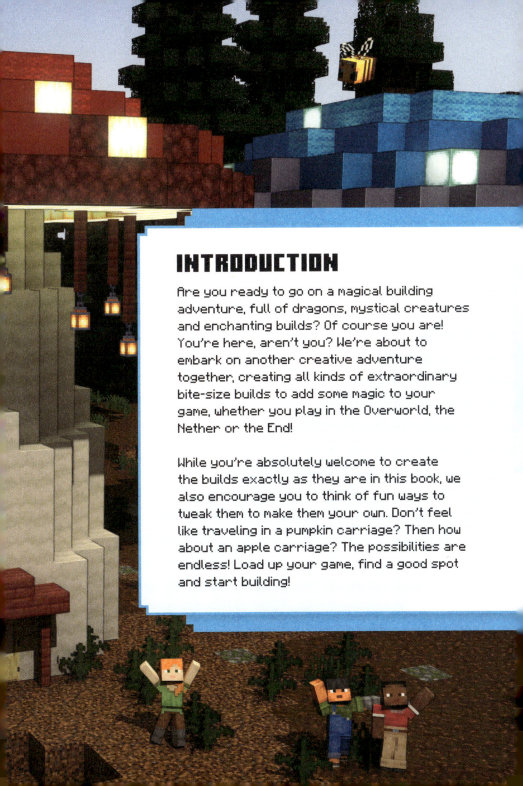

INTRODUCTION

Are you ready to go on a magical building adventure, full of dragons, mystical creatures and enchanting builds? Of course you are! You're here, aren't you? We're about to embark on another creative adventure together, creating all kinds of extraordinary bite-size builds to add some magic to your game, whether you play in the Overworld, the Nether or the End!

While you're absolutely welcome to create the builds exactly as they are in this book, we also encourage you to think of fun ways to tweak them to make them your own. Don't feel like traveling in a pumpkin carriage? Then how about an apple carriage? The possibilities are endless! Load up your game, find a good spot and start building!

GENERAL BUILD TIPS

Check out all the amazing builds in this book! There's really something for everyone, no matter your skill level. You can start with the easy builds or dive straight into one of the more complex builds. The choice is yours! Here are some tips to help you get started.

CREATIVE MODE

We recommend that you use Creative mode for these builds. With unlimited access to all the blocks in the game and instant block removal, Creative mode is the easiest way to build in Minecraft. If you like a challenge, each structure can be built in Survival mode, but be warned – it will take a lot more time and preparation!

BUILD PREPARATION

Before starting a build, take a moment to look at the instructions. Consider where you want to place the structure and how much space you will need to complete it. You'll need to give yourself plenty of room to build!

TEMPORARY BLOCKS

Temporary building blocks are great for counting out spaces or placing floating items. Using temporary blocks will also help you with tricky block placement!

Count the dimensions using different colored blocks. This row represents 11 blocks wide: 5 green + 6 yellow.

Use temporary blocks to help place floating blocks.

HOTBARS

Most builds use lots of different materials. You can prepare your blocks in the hotbar before starting for quick access, and if you don't have enough space, you can save up to nine hotbars in the inventory window.

BLOCK PLACEMENT

Placing a block beside an interactive one, such as an enchanting table, can be tricky. By clicking to place a block, you'll activate the interactive one instead. Thankfully, there is a trick to avoid this! Crouch first and then click to place your block. Simple!

7

MAGIC MIRROR

Magic mirror on the wall, who's the bravest of them a— Wait, no! I wanted to be told I'm brave, not have to prove it in the Nether! Eek — let me out, I'm scared! Build your own magic mirror with a twist and see if any of your friends stray too close in the hope of gaining a compliment.

DIFFICULTY:
★☆☆☆☆
🕐 15 mins

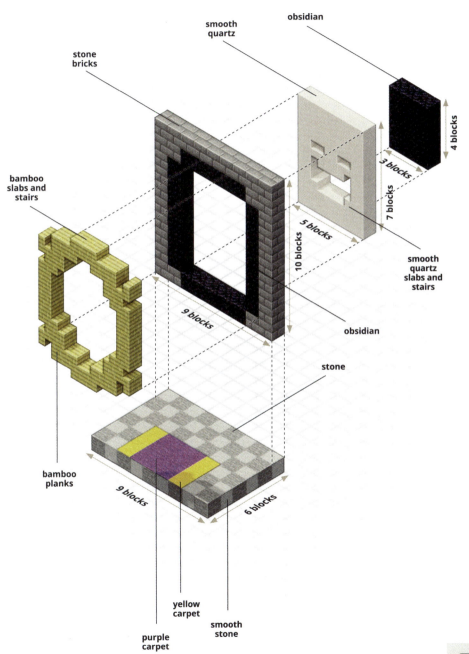

MERMAID LAGOON

Whether you want to build a beautiful water feature near your base, live like a magical mermaid or just have somewhere pretty to do your fishing, this build will make the perfect enchanting addition to your Overworld. So what are you waiting for? Dive right into this mer-mazing build!

DIFFICULTY: ★★★☆☆
🕒 30 mins

1

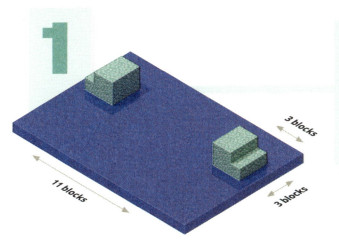

In a space above the water, use prismarine blocks to build the start of your archway 11 blocks apart. Start with one 3x3 square on either side, then top each with a 2x3 block to make stairs, facing outward.

2

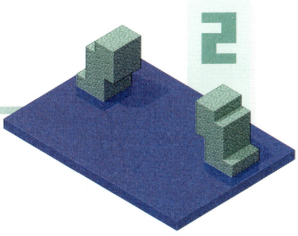

Add another 3x3 layer of prismarine blocks above each, 1 block in toward the middle. Then build another layer of 2x3 blocks on top.

3

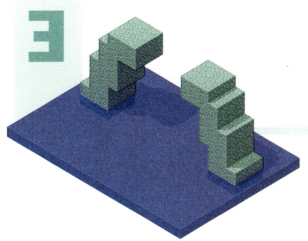

Continue to build your arch inward, adding a 3x4 layer of prismarine, followed by a 3x3 layer above it.

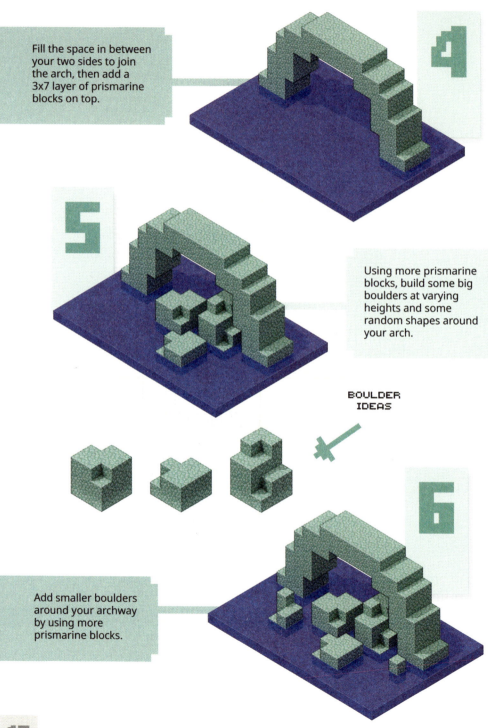

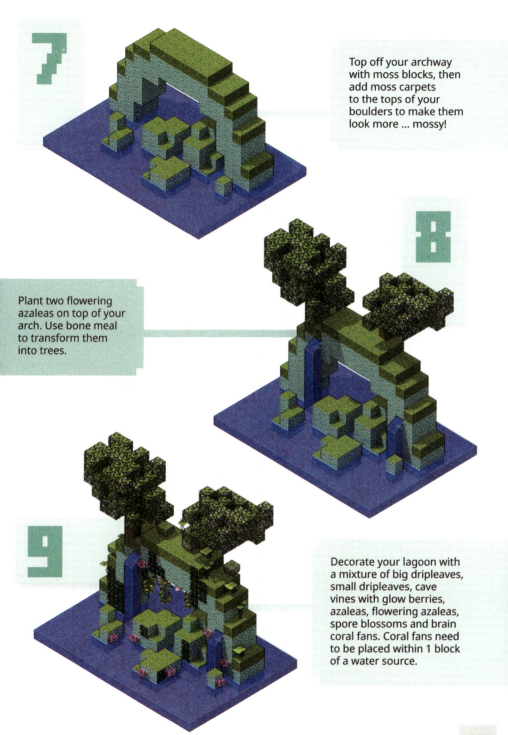

7 Top off your archway with moss blocks, then add moss carpets to the tops of your boulders to make them look more ... mossy!

8 Plant two flowering azaleas on top of your arch. Use bone meal to transform them into trees.

9 Decorate your lagoon with a mixture of big dripleaves, small dripleaves, cave vines with glow berries, azaleas, flowering azaleas, spore blossoms and brain coral fans. Coral fans need to be placed within 1 block of a water source.

GIANT BEANSTALK

Fee-fi-fo-fum, I hear the hiss of a creeper — RUN! Climb up and up ... and up this giant beanstalk to the ultimate base in the sky. Not even creepers can be bothered to follow you up here. Just keep your base fully lit, and you'll be safe from harm — unless you fall off ...

DIFFICULTY:
★★★★★
🕐 1 hr

1

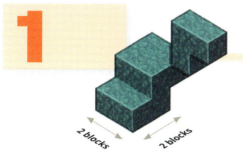

2 blocks · 2 blocks

Pick a block for your beanstalk – we went for warped wart blocks – and start building it. First, add a 2x2 square, then add another one a step up. Add an upside-down L shape for a leaf.

2

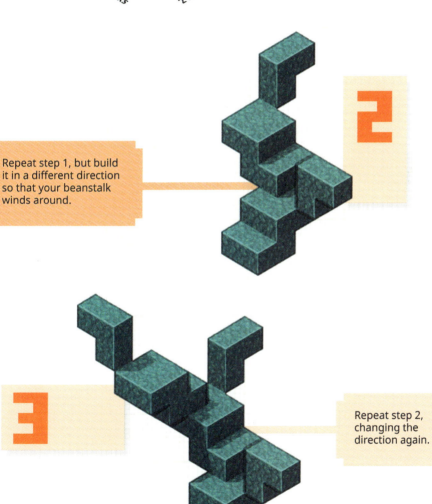

Repeat step 1, but build it in a different direction so that your beanstalk winds around.

3

Repeat step 2, changing the direction again.

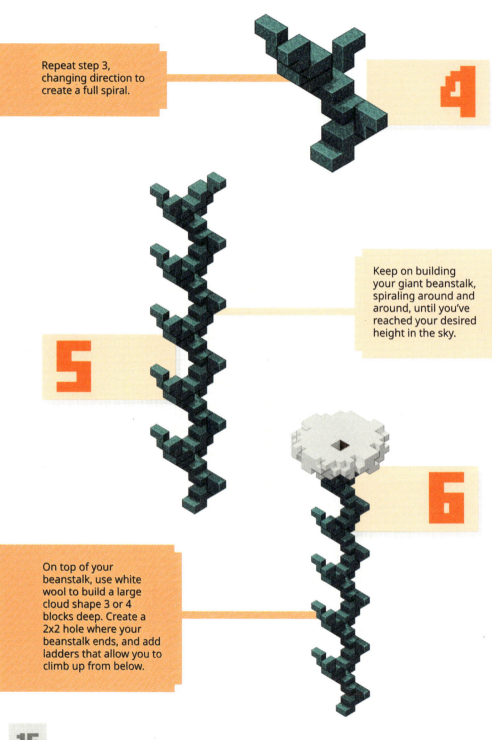

Repeat step 3, changing direction to create a full spiral.

4

Keep on building your giant beanstalk, spiraling around and around, until you've reached your desired height in the sky.

5

On top of your beanstalk, use white wool to build a large cloud shape 3 or 4 blocks deep. Create a 2x2 hole where your beanstalk ends, and add ladders that allow you to climb up from below.

6

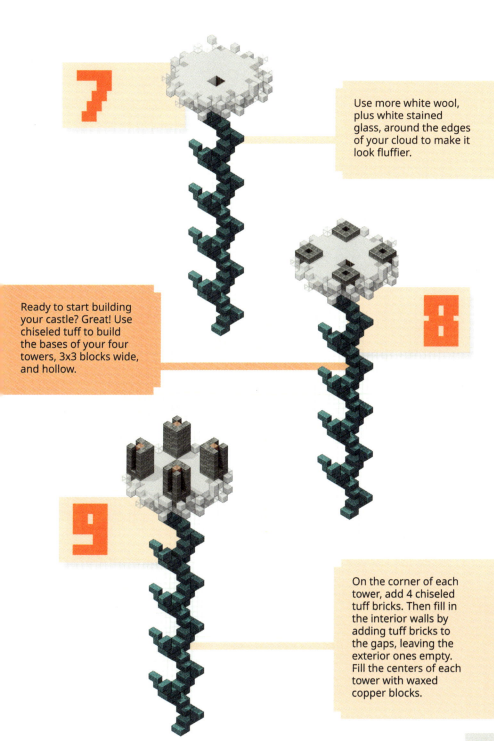

7 Use more white wool, plus white stained glass, around the edges of your cloud to make it look fluffier.

8 Ready to start building your castle? Great! Use chiseled tuff to build the bases of your four towers, 3x3 blocks wide, and hollow.

9 On the corner of each tower, add 4 chiseled tuff bricks. Then fill in the interior walls by adding tuff bricks to the gaps, leaving the exterior ones empty. Fill the centers of each tower with waxed copper blocks.

17

Add a tuff brick block to the top of the gaps in each tower, and place a tuff brick stair beneath. Then add a layer of waxed copper blocks to all towers.

10

All of the coolest castles have turrets, so let's add those next. On the sides of each corner of your towers, place an upside-down tuff brick stair with an upright one on top of it. Then add a tuff brick slab in between them all.

11

Begin to build the walls of your castle by adding a pillar in the center of the tower walls that are facing each other. Each pillar consists of 1 chiseled tuff brick block with 2 tuff blocks on top.

12

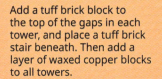

18

13

At the front of the castle, add upside-down tuff brick stairs to both pillars, facing each other. Then on every other side, build a 3x3 wall in the middle, in line with the towers, using a mixture of tuff bricks and tuff blocks.

14

Finish the arch above your entrance with tuff brick slabs and stairs, then use the same blocks to create turrets along your walls.

15

Complete your castle with some decorations! You can build flags with a waxed copper block, topped with 2 tuff brick walls and a flag of cyan and orange wool blocks. You can also add banners in the same colors around your towers.

19

MAGICIAN'S HAT

What could be more magical than a giant magician's hat with bunny ears poking out the top? Actual rabbits spawning from it, of course! This build will have you hopping with joy every time you leave your base! Just be sure to put a fence around your carrot patch before the rabbits eat them all.

DIFFICULTY: ★☆☆☆☆

🕒 15 mins

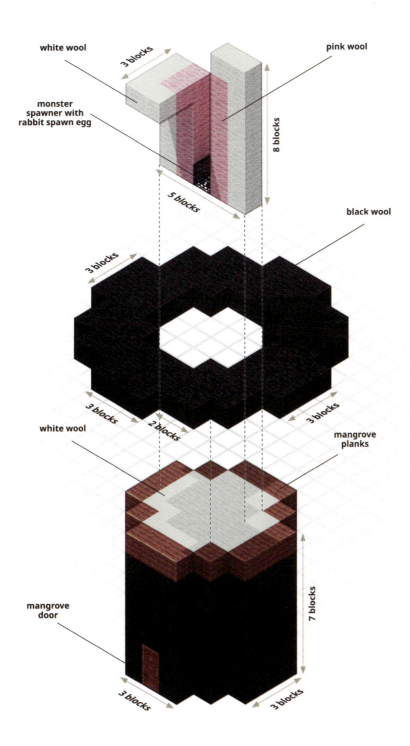

FEROCIOUS DRAGON

Nothing says "Stay away from my base, or else!" quite like a fire-breathing dragon on your doorstep! This build is the perfect security system for treasure hoarders and brave solo adventurers. If anyone strays too close, they'll soon be running from this dragon's fireballs.

DIFFICULTY:
★★★☆☆
🕒 30 mins

1

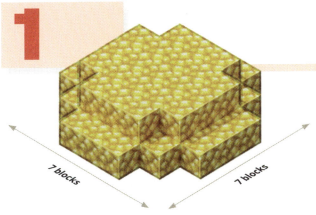

Build a base for your dragon statue using blocks of raw gold – don't worry, no one will be brave enough to steal it! Build the first layer in a rough circle, 7 blocks wide. Then add another layer on top, 1 block in.

7 blocks

7 blocks

2

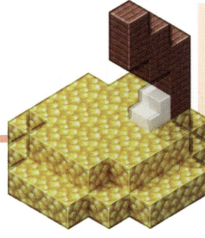

Build the first leg of your dragon using mangrove planks in a zigzag formation, with a quartz stair in front for its talons.

3

Build the second leg, zigzagging away from the first leg with the same mixture of blocks. Both legs should be the same height and should end next to each other with 1 block of space between them.

23

Now it's time to start building the body! Between the legs, 1 block wide, build the body shape with mangrove planks and slabs. It should be square in the back and have a hook where the neck begins.

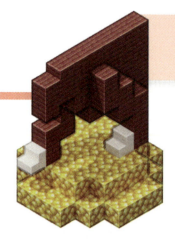

SIDE

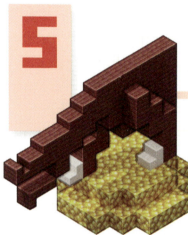

Finish the neck with mangrove planks. Build the head and open mouth with a mixture of mangrove planks, stairs and slabs.

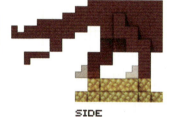

SIDE

Build fearsome horns made from 2 quartz stairs with a quartz slab on top, on both sides of its head. Add polished blackstone buttons for eyes. Then place a dispenser in its mouth with a mangrove sign on either side.

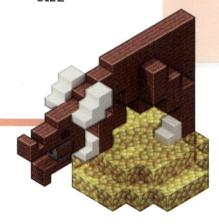

24

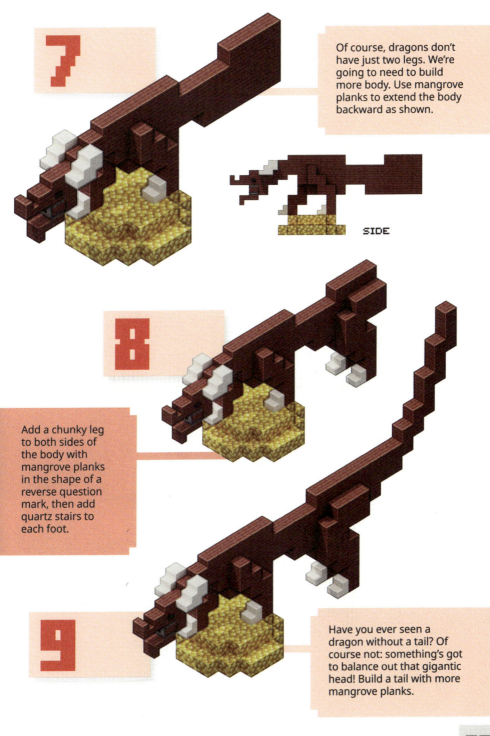

7 Of course, dragons don't have just two legs. We're going to need to build more body. Use mangrove planks to extend the body backward as shown.

SIDE

8 Add a chunky leg to both sides of the body with mangrove planks in the shape of a reverse question mark, then add quartz stairs to each foot.

9 Have you ever seen a dragon without a tail? Of course not: something's got to balance out that gigantic head! Build a tail with more mangrove planks.

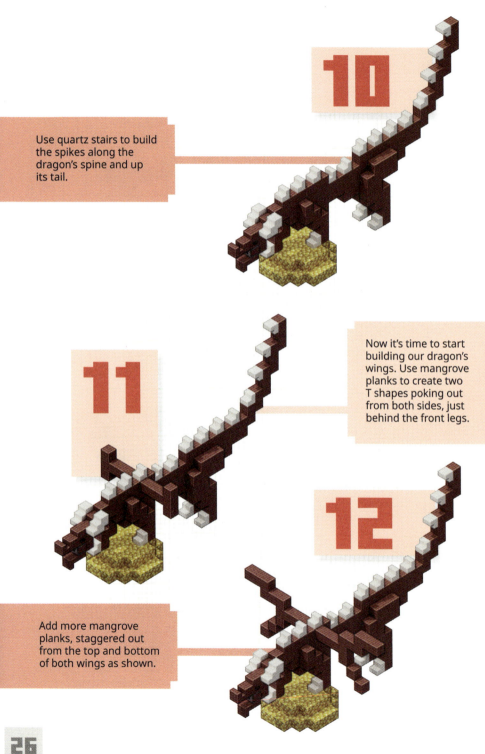

Use quartz stairs to build the spikes along the dragon's spine and up its tail.

10

Now it's time to start building our dragon's wings. Use mangrove planks to create two T shapes poking out from both sides, just behind the front legs.

11

12

Add more mangrove planks, staggered out from the top and bottom of both wings as shown.

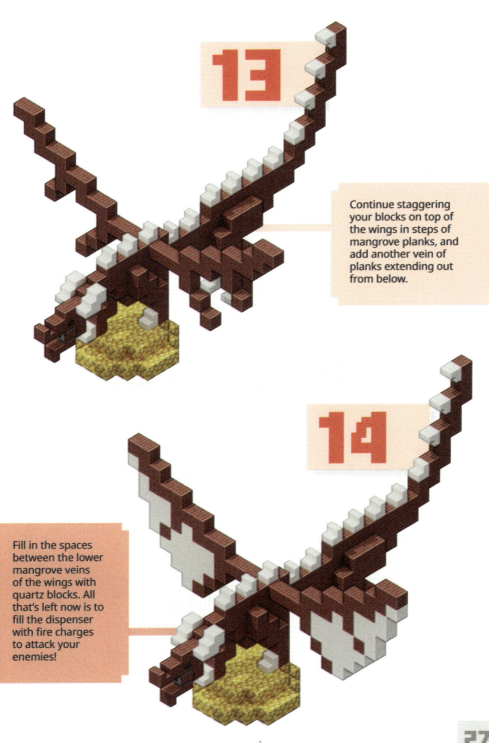

13 Continue staggering your blocks on top of the wings in steps of mangrove planks, and add another vein of planks extending out from below.

14 Fill in the spaces between the lower mangrove veins of the wings with quartz blocks. All that's left now is to fill the dispenser with fire charges to attack your enemies!

BUBBLEGUM COTTAGE

Isn't this the sweetest base you've ever seen? If bubblegum cottagecore is your vibe, then this is the build for you. If it's not, then why not try mixing up the blocks until you've got a style that works for you? If you prefer a witchy vibe, give deepslate and mangrove planks a go.

DIFFICULTY:
★★★★★
🕒 40 mins

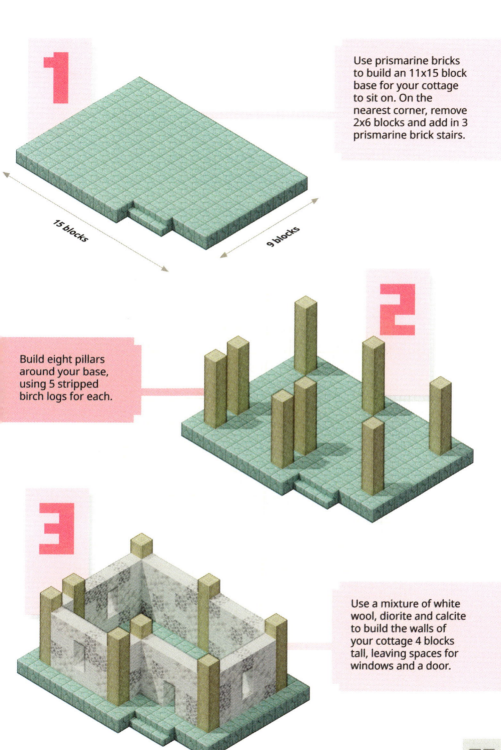

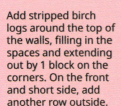

Add stripped birch logs around the top of the walls, filling in the spaces and extending out by 1 block on the corners. On the front and short side, add another row outside.

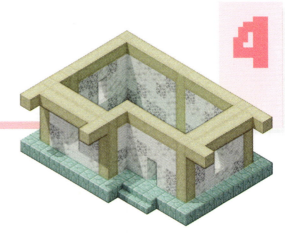

Use a mixture of white wool, diorite and calcite to build two triangular walls on the front and side. Make sure you leave a space in the middle for a window.

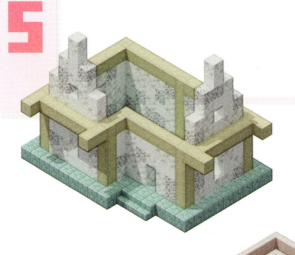

Use cherry planks and stairs to build the roof, staggering up in line with the walls and meeting in the middle to make an L shape.

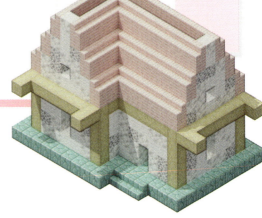

7

Add prismarine brick blocks and stairs along the top and around all of the roof's edges. Add a lantern beneath a stair at the peak of each end of the roof.

8

To build your doorway, first add a birch door to the space. On both sides, add a prismarine brick wall with a cherry fence and a cherry slab on top. Add a cherry plank between the two slabs to complete the archway.

9

Add window panes to your windows, then on the bottom floor, add a cherry door on either side to look like shutters. Build planters using cherry trapdoors around grass blocks.

31

10

On the corners where the pillars are, add a prismarine brick wall with cherry fences on top.

11

Add birch trapdoors on both sides of the upstairs windows to look like shutters. Place more lanterns under the birch log blocks.

12

Use birch fences to build an adorable weather vane on your roof. Then decorate your build with a mixture of flowering azalea leaves, azalea leaves and vines.

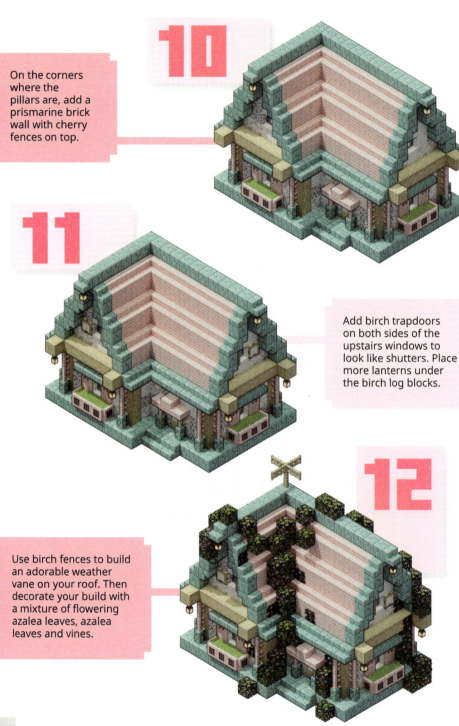

13

Fence off your garden using birch fences with lanterns on the corners.

14

Fill your cottage garden with peonies, flowering azaleas and cherry leaves on birch fences.

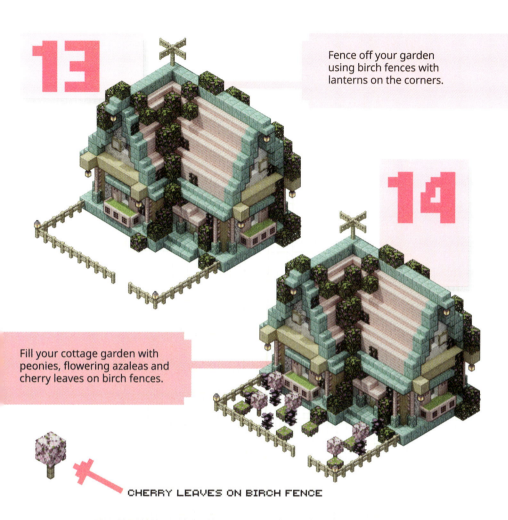

CHERRY LEAVES ON BIRCH FENCE

INTERIOR

Continue your cottage theme inside, using a mixture of barrels, stripped birch logs, cherry fences, lanterns, flower pots, bookshelves and more to make it look homey. You could even put birch fences inside decorated pots with cherry leaves on top to look like little indoor trees!

ENCHANTING TOWER

Unlock your magic and embrace the witchy vibes with this spellbinding build! Keep all of your precious mystical books safe and sound at the top of a tower, where you can experience the elements and take in the views while you work your magic to enchant all of your items.

DIFFICULTY:
★★★☆☆
◷ 30 mins

1

Using waxed oxidized cut copper blocks, build your tower 14 blocks tall and 5 blocks wide, with the corners missing. Leave a 2-block space for a door.

5 blocks 5 blocks

2

Add a spruce door, then a ladder climbing up the middle of your tower.

3

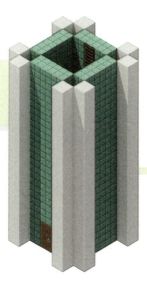

Once you're happy with the shape of your tower, use quartz pillars to build two pillars on each corner.

35

Add a square roof of quartz blocks, extending out as far as your quartz pillars. Leave a hole where your ladder ends, and pop a spruce trapdoor on it. Place quartz stairs on each corner, with a lantern dangling beneath them.

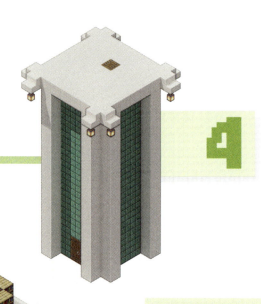

4

5

ROTATED 180°

It wouldn't be an enchanting tower without your enchanting equipment! Add an enchanting table, then surround it on three sides with bookshelves.

Begin building your decorative arches. First, add 2 quartz pillar blocks to each corner, then place a set of quartz stair block on top. On the sides of the stairs, add 2 more upside-down stairs with a quartz pillar on top of each.

6

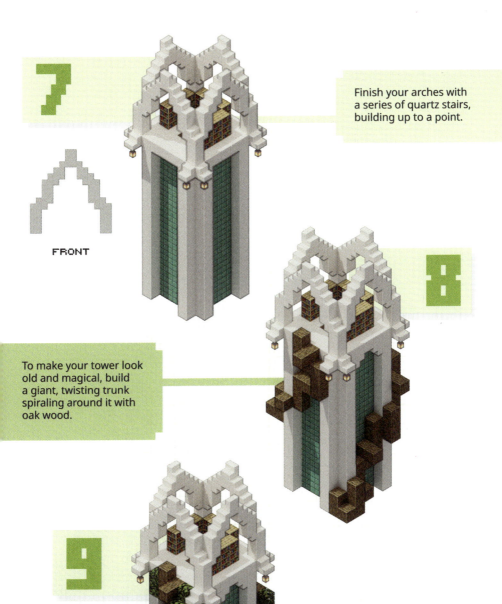

7

FRONT

Finish your arches with a series of quartz stairs, building up to a point.

8

To make your tower look old and magical, build a giant, twisting trunk spiraling around it with oak wood.

9

Finish by decorating your wooden trunk with oak leaves. And you're done!

37

PUMPKIN CARRIAGE

Bibbidi-bobbidi-build this enchanting pumpkin carriage! It won't get you very far, but it will keep you safe from wicked witches and the occasional zombie. Just be sure to pack plenty of pumpkin pies, as you'll have to wait well past midnight before it's safe to venture outside again.

DIFFICULTY:
★★☆☆☆
⏲ 20 mins

1

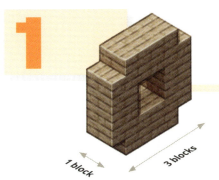

Place 4 jungle planks in a circle with a hole in the middle, and then add jungle stairs to each corner to create your first wheel.

2

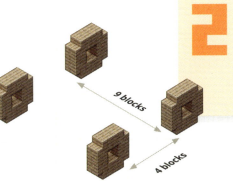

Leave a gap of 9 blocks, and then repeat step 1 to build another wheel shape. Leave 4 blocks behind them and build two more wheels.

3

Use green concrete blocks to build curving vines connecting the front and back wheels to each other on the insides.

4

Use more green concrete to connect both sides of the wheels to each other.

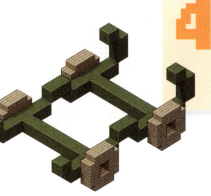

5

In the center of your carriage, use orange wool to build a square. It should have a 1-block gap around it.

6

Use more orange wool to build edges around your first square, 1 block up and out, leaving off the corners.

7

Another block up and outside of the previous layer, build 4-block-high walls with orange wool in a circle, including the corners. Add 2 acacia doors to the side of your pumpkin so you can get in.

8

Mirror the bottom layers of your pumpkin to build the roof, building 1 block in on both layers.

9

Use green concrete blocks to build a curved stem on top of your pumpkin.

10

Add vines to some edges of your pumpkin carriage to make it look more realistic.

ROYAL FROG

This froggy monarch has been stuck in stone for ages, just waiting for someone to come along and break its curse. In the meantime, it makes a lovely water fountain, don't you think? Add a touch of magic to your pond or water feature by building a ribbiting royal frog fountain of your own!

DIFFICULTY:
★★☆☆☆
🕐 10 mins

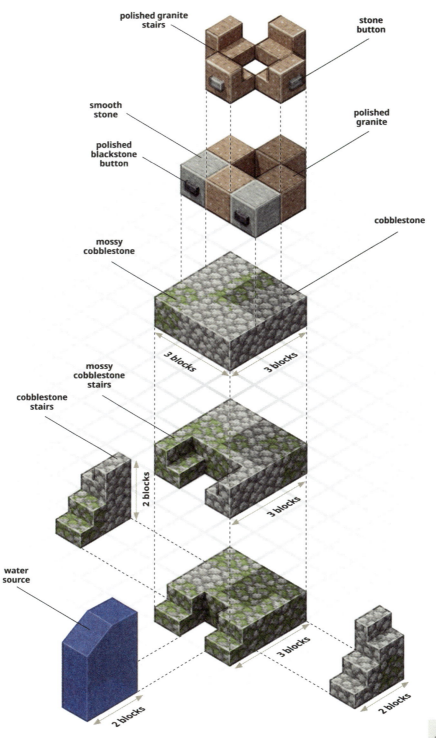

GLOWING MUSHROOM

Whether you want to live a fairy life, always struggle to find your base at night or just want to find a fungi home, this glowing mushroom base is for you. You could even fill an entire forest with these to create a mushroom kingdom – with you as its monarch (or not)!

DIFFICULTY:
★★★★☆
◷ 35 mins

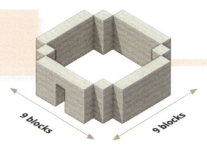

Start by building your mushroom stem, using – you guessed it – mushroom stems in a circular shape, 3 blocks tall. Leave a space for a door at the front.

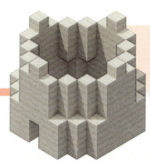

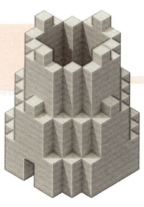

Build your next level 3 blocks tall with more mushroom stems, shifting 1 block in on the corners only. After this, add another block to the middles of the straight edges on your build.

Using more mushroom stems, add another level 4 blocks tall, moving inward on all sides. Again, add another block to the centers of each straight edge.

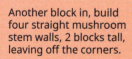
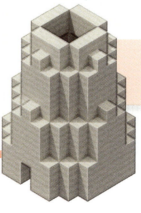

Another block in, build four straight mushroom stem walls, 2 blocks tall, leaving off the corners.

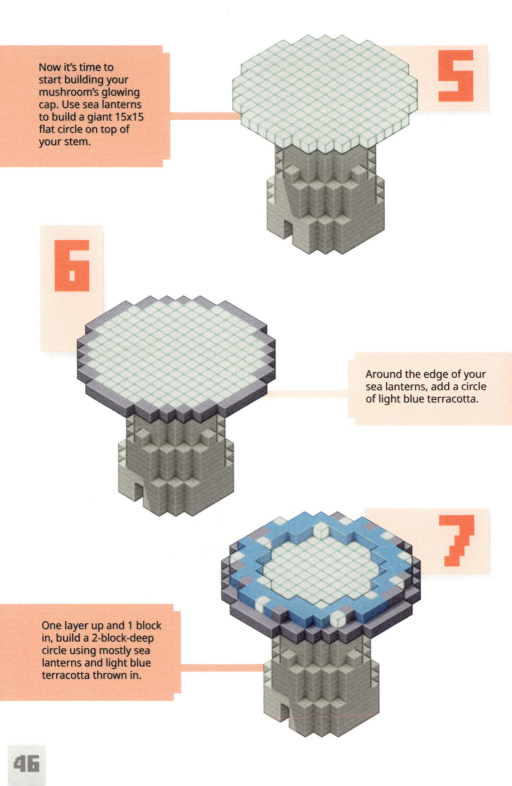

5 Now it's time to start building your mushroom's glowing cap. Use sea lanterns to build a giant 15x15 flat circle on top of your stem.

6 Around the edge of your sea lanterns, add a circle of light blue terracotta.

7 One layer up and 1 block in, build a 2-block-deep circle using mostly sea lanterns and light blue terracotta thrown in.

8

Build the next layer up, 2 blocks in, using mostly the light blue concrete blocks again but with some sea lanterns and light blue wool scattered in it. Make it 2 blocks deep on the straight edges and 1 block deep on the diagonals so that it's circular on the outside and almost square on the inside.

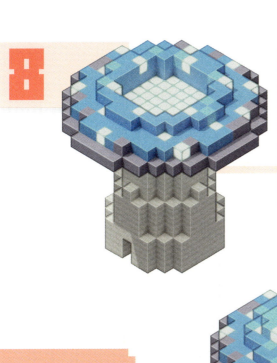

9

Create a final layer above with light blue wool and a few sea lanterns dotted about.

10

It's time to decorate! Add a warped door, then place 2 warped fences on both sides of it. Build an entryway with 2 warped slabs and a warped plank between them. Dangle some soul lanterns from warped fences beneath your mushroom cap.

HOUSE IN A SHOE

What a boot-iful house! Have you ever seen such a feet of architecture before? Why don't you knock your friends and family's socks off by building this ab-shoe-lutely charming base?

DIFFICULTY:
★★★★☆
⏱ 40 mins

1

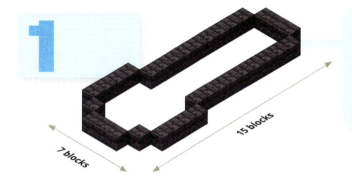

Build the sole of your boot with polished blackstone bricks in a rough foot shape, 5 blocks wide at the back and widening to 7 blocks at the front.

7 blocks

15 blocks

2

Use spruce planks to create walls 3 blocks tall, following the layout of the sole, except for in the middle, where you'll keep the 7-block width for an additional 5 blocks. Leave holes for glass panes and one hole in the side for a door.

3

Build your boot 2 blocks higher with spruce planks. Stagger the edges inward at the front to fill in the rounded toe section. Leave a hole at the back for the ankle section.

Build a circular wall around the ankle section of the boot, 4 blocks tall with spruce planks. To both sides, add a window with a glass pane.

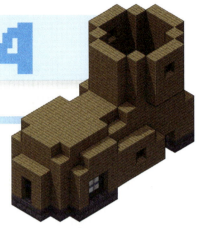

Add a pillar of stone brick walls to both corners of the ankle section. Use brick blocks and slabs to create a staggered roof on top, leaving a hole in one side.

Around your doorway, use cracked stone bricks as well as stone brick blocks and stairs to create an archway. Then add an oak door.

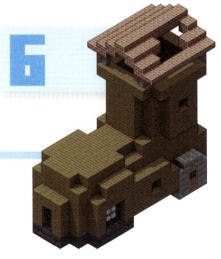

7

Use oak trapdoors around grass blocks to create some planters beneath the windows, and add a couple more for shutters. Add some flowers to your planters – we used pink petals.

8

Use chains to create lines along the top of your boot base to look like shoelaces.

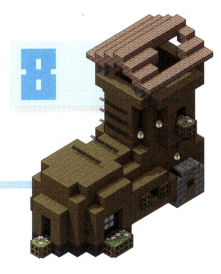

9

Use oak leaves to fill in the hole in the roof, and have them trail down the side of the boot. Finish with some lanterns dangling from chains.

ALEBRIJE STATUES

Take some inspiration from Mexican folklore and populate your Overworld with these beautiful statues. The trick is to include lots of color to create unique-looking animals – your creativity is key. We've given you some inspiration, but make whatever alebrijes you want!

DIFFICULTY:
★☆☆☆☆
30 mins

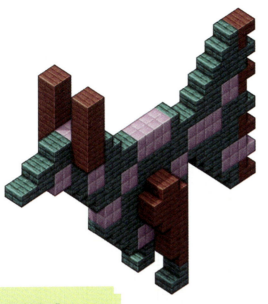

This alebrije is like a colorful, horned chicken. Egg-cellent!

First, build the flat center of your alebrije. Use purpur blocks, mangrove stairs and warped planks, slabs and stairs to make the rough shape of a side-on chicken. Take a step back and check that you are happy with the base of your build.

1

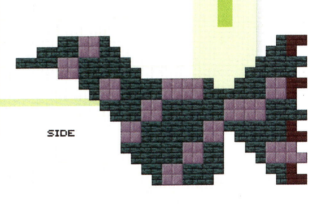

SIDE

2

SIDE

Next, use mangrove planks and stairs along with warped stairs to create the legs and horns. Do this for both sides of your build.

What's cooler than a multicolored horse? A multicolored horse with wings, of course!

First, build the flat center of your statue in the rough shape of a horse's head, body and tail. Use warped planks and stairs, bamboo mosaic blocks and stairs, and smooth red sandstone blocks, slabs and stairs.

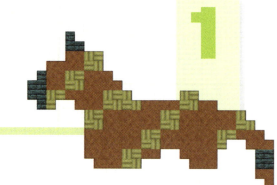

1

SIDE

2

SIDE

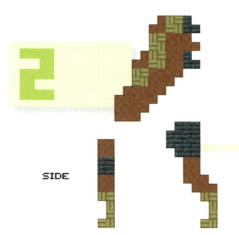

On each side of the body, add a leg and a wing using a mixture of the same blocks.

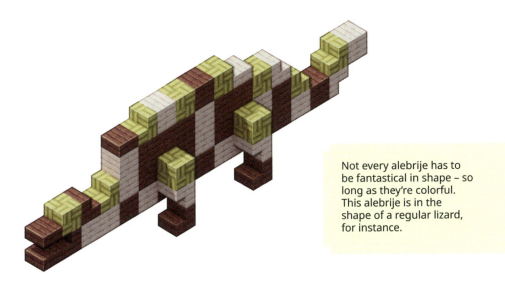

Not every alebrije has to be fantastical in shape – so long as they're colorful. This alebrije is in the shape of a regular lizard, for instance.

1

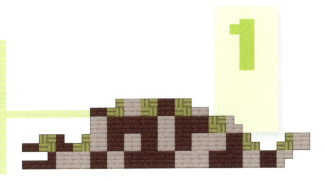

Start again by building the flat center of your alebrije – this time in the shape of a lizard's head, body and tail. Use bamboo mosaic blocks and stairs, mangrove planks, slabs and stairs, and cherry planks, slabs and stairs to create this cool and colorful statue.

SIDE

2

Next, add a leg to either side of your alebrije, using the same mixture of blocks. And you're done! What other statues will you build?

SIDE

BANANA-SPLIT BASE

This build is magical to the eyes and the taste buds! OK, so ice cream doesn't exist in Minecraft, but you can still whip up a legen-dairy house for you to kick back, relax and chill in. And the cherry on top of this sundae is that you can switch out the colors to match your chosen theme!

DIFFICULTY:
★★★☆☆
🕒 25 mins

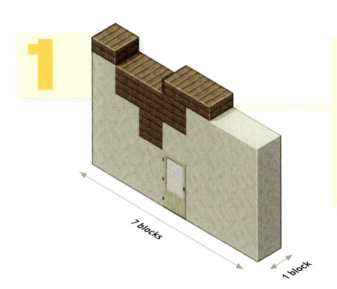

Use smooth sandstone blocks to create a wall 7 blocks wide. Place spruce planks and slabs on the top and in the middle, replacing some of your smooth sandstone. This will look like gooey, melted chocolate. Place a birch door so you can get inside your house!

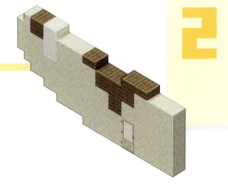

With smooth sandstone blocks, slabs and stairs, extend your wall, staggering the bottom upward to create a curved shape. Add spruce blocks and slabs for more chocolate sauce, and add quartz blocks for whipped cream.

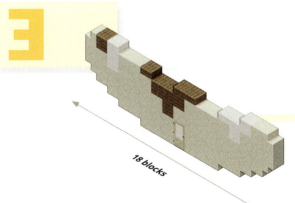

Repeat step 2 on the other side to extend the banana shape. Decorate with more quartz blocks.

Repeat steps 1, 2 and 3 to build another banana-split wall 5 blocks behind your first. Add a wall of white concrete blocks on both sides of your build, extending inward to fill in the holes at the bottom of your banana walls.

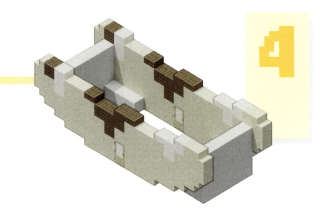

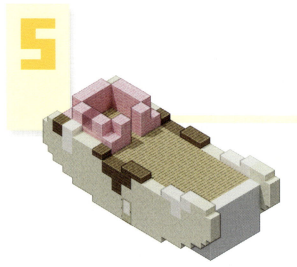

Fill your banana-split with a layer of oak planks. Now it's time to create your first ice cream scoop! Build a 5x5 square of pink wool, leaving a space for a door. Add another layer on top, leaving off the corners, and add a pink stained glass block at the front for a window.

Finish the ice cream scoop with pink wool by extending the walls up another layer, then adding a 3x3 roof on top. On one side, leave a gap of 2 blocks for a little doorway.

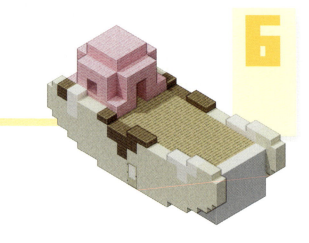

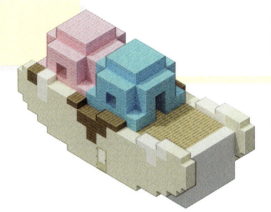

Repeat steps 5 and 6, this time using light blue wool and a light blue stained glass block. Remember to leave a 2-block gap for another doorway.

Repeat steps 5 and 6 for a final time, using yellow wool and a yellow stained glass block. Leave a 2-block gap for the doorway. You have three delicious-looking ice cream scoops!

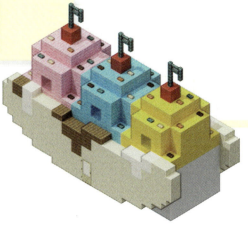

Finish by placing a red wool block in the center of each ice cream scoop. Add warped fences for cherry stems. Then for sprinkles, use warped, birch, crimson and acacia buttons. Now it's time to dig in. Wait, no – time to *move* in!

FLOATING TEA PARTY

Be our guest and dive into this tea-rrific build! Not only does it have a fun pool with a waterfall you can swim up and ride down, but it also has a floating hideout in the teapot for when unwanted guests show up for your tea party. Stop crashing the party, creepers!

DIFFICULTY: ★★★★☆

🕐 35 mins

1

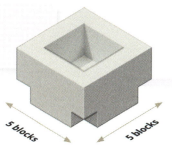

Let's start by building the teacup swimming pool. For the base, use white concrete to build a 5x5 square with the corners missing. Then build up the edges by 2 blocks, including the corners this time.

2

To the outside center of each wall, add 1 white concrete block, then add a row of 3 more on top. Add another block to the place where each wall meets. Then add another layer on top, alternating between yellow concrete and light blue terracotta blocks.

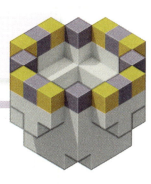

3

Build a handle with light blue terracotta, then add a ladder on the side so you can climb up to your pool.

4

Fill your teacup by placing water from each side, facing in, until the water stops flowing. Now all you're missing is your teapot!

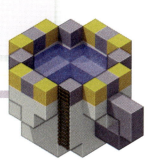

5

Above and to the side of your teacup, build a floating platform with a 3x3 square of white concrete. Add light blue terracotta and yellow concrete around the outside. To do this, you'll need to build a pillar and remove it afterward.

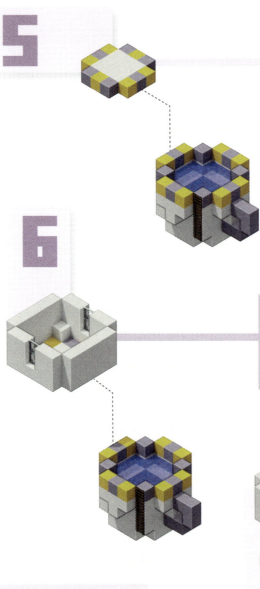

6

One layer above, use more white concrete to build walls around the outside, 3 blocks high and with spaces for glass panes. Add blocks inside over the holes in the corners.

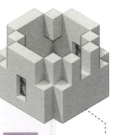

7

One block in on the corners, add another two layers of white concrete, leaving a space for an entrance on the side.

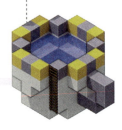

62

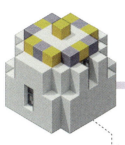

Build the lid for your teapot with white concrete in the middle and more yellow concrete and light blue terracotta around the outside. Top with a yellow concrete block.

Use light blue terracotta to build a handle and spout on your teapot. The spout should jut out above your teacup.

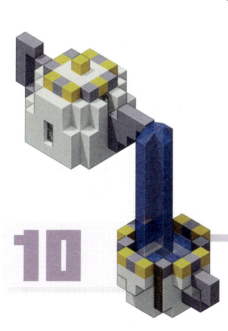

Add a water source block at the end of the spout to create a waterfall. You can swim up this to enter the teapot. Time for tea!

DRAGON ROLLER COASTER

Calling all thrill-seekers – this roller coaster build is for you! Start by jumping aboard a minecart in the dragon's mouth, then ride along its curving body, up and down until you plummet back into its mouth ... then do it all over again! Do you have the guts to take a ride? *Gulp!*

DIFFICULTY:
★★★★☆

🕒 45 mins

1

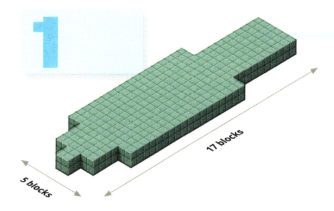

Let's start by building our fearsome dragon's head! Use oxidized cut copper blocks to build the bottom of the head. It should be pointed on the front and 5 blocks wide, narrowing to 3 blocks wide for the neck.

2

At the beginning of the neck, build 2-block-tall walls with oxidized cut copper, extending 5 blocks toward the head, adding 1 single block to each end. Add 6 bone blocks for teeth. Then add powered rails along the center of the build, with 1 regular rail at the end. Place redstone torches on both sides: between the teeth and along the neck.

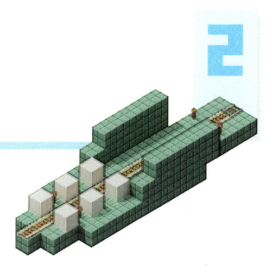

3

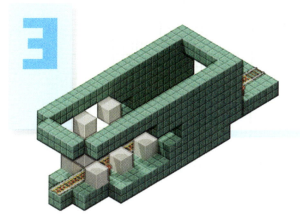

Use more oxidized cut copper to begin building the dragon's upper jaw, extending forward to where the mouth below is 3-blocks wide.

Build the top of your dragon's head with more oxidized cut copper, adding a nose with black concrete for nostrils. For the eyes, use a black concrete block and an ochre froglight.

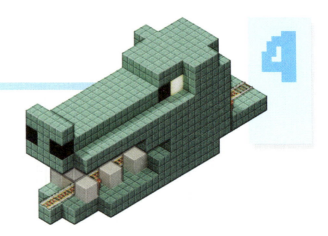

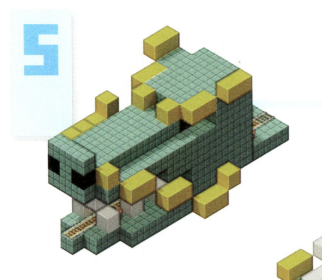

Give your dragon some awesome eyebrows and whiskers with yellow concrete blocks.

Use bone blocks again to give your dragon some epic horns.

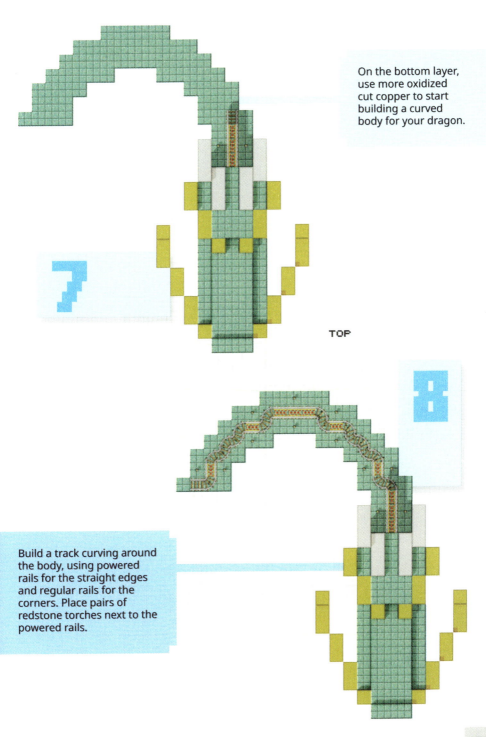

On the bottom layer, use more oxidized cut copper to start building a curved body for your dragon.

TOP

Build a track curving around the body, using powered rails for the straight edges and regular rails for the corners. Place pairs of redstone torches next to the powered rails.

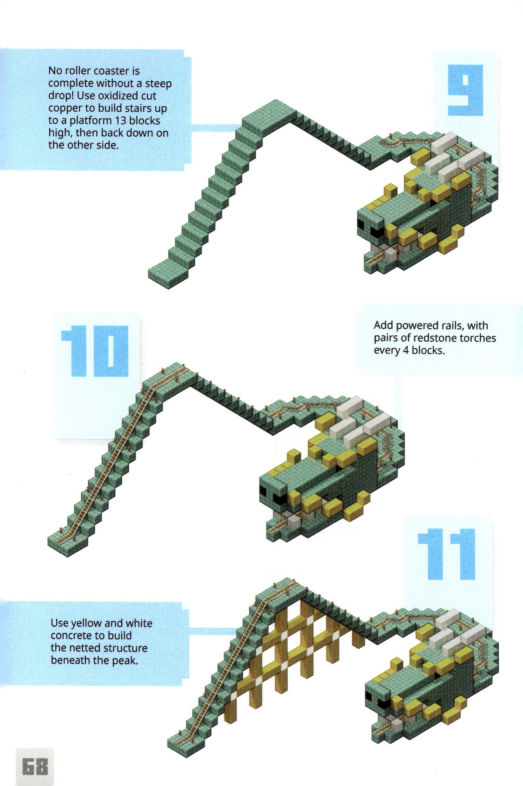

9 No roller coaster is complete without a steep drop! Use oxidized cut copper to build stairs up to a platform 13 blocks high, then back down on the other side.

10 Add powered rails, with pairs of redstone torches every 4 blocks.

11 Use yellow and white concrete to build the netted structure beneath the peak.

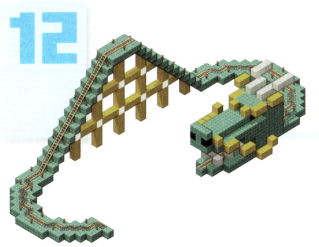

Curve your roller coaster around, mirroring the shape you built in steps 7 and 8. Add the regular rails and powered rails, and then place more redstone torches.

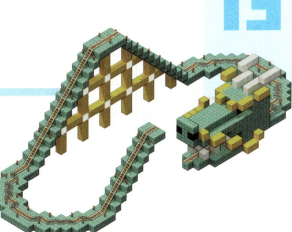

Build another steep drop using oxidized cut copper blocks, extending up 8 blocks. With the right spacing, this will drop you right into the dragon's mouth! Add more powered rails and redstone torches.

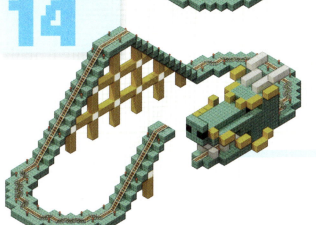

Finish your roller coaster by using yellow and white concrete to build the supporting structure below your final ascent.

SPELLBOOK SHOP

Friends and hostile mobs will flock from all around the Overworld to get their hands on your spellbinding books. But you might want to be a bit selective about who you let in. We suggest you don't send any handwritten invitations to witches. You don't want to give them ideas for more pesky potions to throw!

DIFFICULTY:
★★★★☆
🕒 40 mins

1

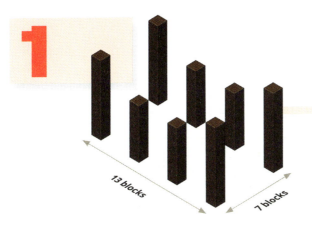

Build eight pillars of dark oak logs, 4 blocks tall for the inner pillars and 6 blocks tall for the outer pillars. Add the first row of four pillars with 3 blocks between them, and then place the second row 6 blocks back.

2

Place stone bricks between each of the pillars, leaving a 1-block space in the front center. Then add stone brick stairs around the outside edges at the base of each pillar.

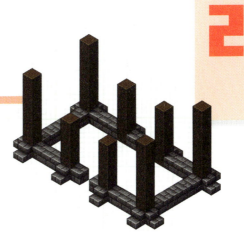

3

Place stripped birch logs 2 blocks high to fill in the walls between the pillars. Leave three spaces for windows, and add a block above the doorway at the front.

Use glass panes for windows, and add a dark oak door.

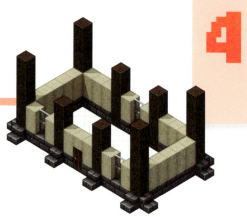

4

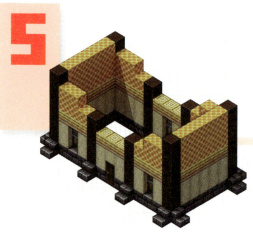

5

Add a layer of bee nests between all the pillars. Then use honeycomb blocks to fill in the sides between the tall pillars, and add staggered walls to the other side of each of the corners.

Use brown concrete blocks to fill in the roof, following the shape of the walls beneath it. Extend it 1 block out on every side. Then replace the corner blocks of your roof with gold blocks.

6

7

Use smooth quartz blocks and slabs to add another layer to your roof. Now it looks like the pages of a book!

8

The mark of a fancy hardcover is a ribbon bookmark – use red wool to add one above your door. Light up your build by adding lanterns beneath the gold blocks on the corners.

9

Use a mixture of colored glass panes and blocks to create winding lines coming from the top. Not only does this look like magic, but it will also make your shop visible from a distance for eager customers to spot!

GENIE-LAMP BOAT

Ahoy, there! Who wouldn't wish for this in-genie-ous build?! If you want to live like a genie, then look no further. What this houseboat lacks in space, it more than makes up for with style! Wandering traders will be lining up for blocks in hopes of gaining wishes ... but maybe watch out for the drowned?

DIFFICULTY:
★★★☆☆
🕒 25 mins

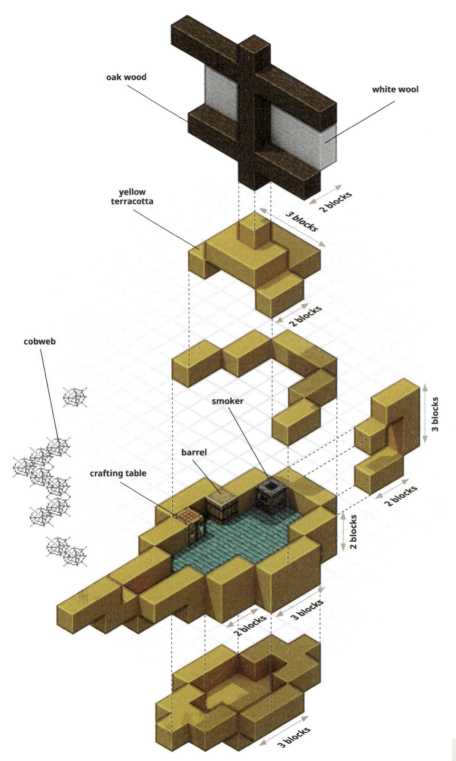

EMERALD APARTMENTS

No emerald city is complete without an emerald apartment complex, and no emerald apartment complex is complete without plenty of emerald! Once you've built it, I'm sure you'll have lots of villagers willing to be your tenants. Just be sure they don't run off with your emerald blocks!

DIFFICULTY:
★★★☆☆
⏲ 45 mins

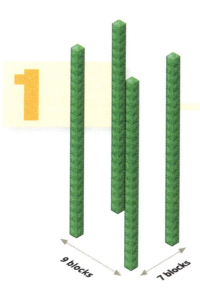

1 Build four pillars, 23 blocks tall, using emerald blocks.

9 blocks
7 blocks

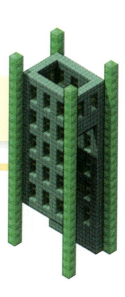

2 Starting 2 blocks below the tops of your pillars, use waxed oxidized cut copper to build the walls of your tower within your pillars, with windows spaced evenly across them. The front wall should come down 16 blocks, the back wall to the ground, and the side walls just 5 blocks. Add lime stained glass panes to all your windows.

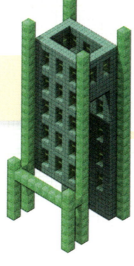

3 Using more emerald blocks, build a 7-block-high arch in front of your tower, and attach it near the top of your original pillars. This will be your grand entrance.

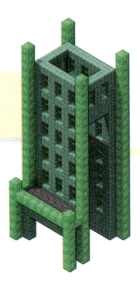

Use cobbled deepslate to fill in the roof of your entrance, then build an arch beneath it with more waxed oxidized cut copper.

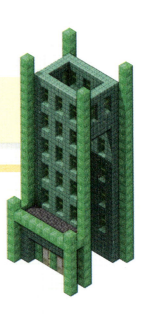

Within the copper arch, set back 1 block, use emerald blocks and birch doors to fill the space and finish your entrance.

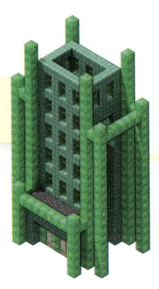

Now we need to build the side wings. Use emerald blocks 18 blocks high to build arches on both sides, connected to the original pillars with a block near the top.

Build the roofs of your wings with cobbled deepslate. Beneath this, fill in the walls with waxed oxidized cut copper, leaving spaces for windows, which you can fill with lime stained glass panes.

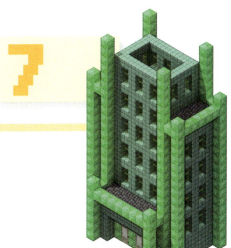

Let's not forget a roof for your main tower! Use cobbled deepslate stairs along both sides, then fill in the middle with cobbled deepslate blocks.

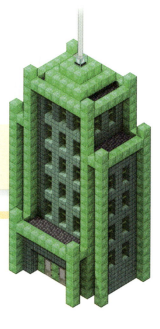

Finish off your epic roof with a 5x5 square of emerald blocks and a 3x3 square on top of that. Then place a beacon in the middle so it can be seen from a distance.

10

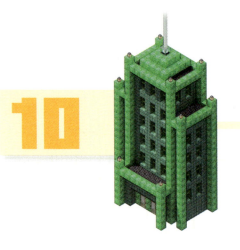

Light up your building with lanterns placed on all of the corners. Ta-da!

11

Of course, no emerald city is complete without a yellow road! Start building a path from your entrance by replacing various grass blocks with gold blocks.

12

Fill in the gaps and make your road wider with a bunch of raw gold blocks, bamboo blocks and stripped bamboo blocks. Doesn't it look more interesting than gold alone?

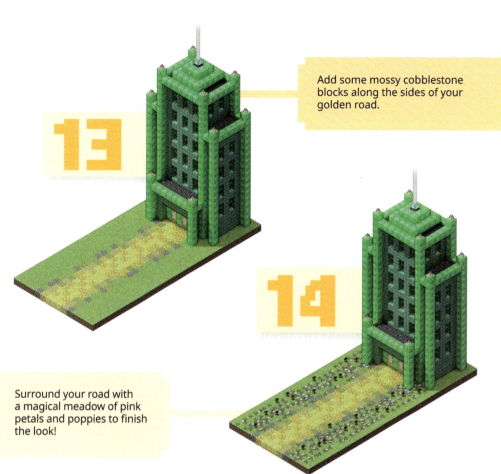

13

Add some mossy cobblestone blocks along the sides of your golden road.

14

Surround your road with a magical meadow of pink petals and poppies to finish the look!

INTERIORS

It's time to create the apartments! Use cobbled deepslate slabs to separate each level. Add a kitchen with a workstation and a crafting table. For a bedroom, add a bed and a sofa made from quartz stairs. Use lime and green carpets for rugs (very fancy). For the attic, use barrels, chests and shulker boxes. Then build two elevator shafts with water. Place a soul sand block beneath one and a magma block beneath the other. Now you can zoom up and down! Finish decorating with lanterns. Who will your new house guests be? Friends or zombies?

FAIRY-TALE PALACE

Live like royalty in your very own magical palace. This build is perfect for customization. If pretty and pink isn't your vibe, then just switch out some blocks for an entirely different theme, such as dark and dangerous or mystical and mysterious. Build it your way!

DIFFICULTY:
★★★★★
⏲ 1 hr

1

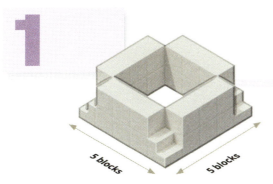

Start building your entrance tower with quartz blocks in a 5x5 square, 2 blocks tall, with the corners missing. Add quartz stairs to the bottom of each corner.

2

Extend your walls up another 4 blocks, changing to smooth quartz. On the front, replace 2 blocks with prismarine walls, then add more of these to the tops of your corners. Build a square of purpur blocks around the top.

3

FRONT

Around the outside of the purpur blocks, alternate between cherry slabs and upside-down cherry stairs. Then use a mixture of cherry planks and stairs to create a staggered roof, ending in a point.

Repeating steps 1, 2 and 3, build a second tower beside your first, leaving 5 blocks between them.

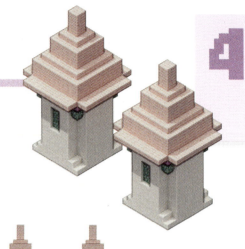

4

5

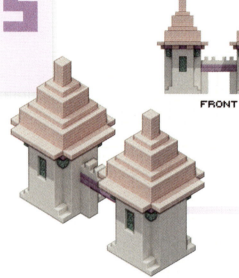

FRONT

Connect your two towers with an arch of quartz and purpur blocks. On top, add 4 quartz stairs with a quartz slab in the middle.

Build walls extending 2 blocks out and 16 blocks back from the side of the towers. Use quartz for the bottom 2 blocks, then smooth quartz for two layers. Top with quartz stairs and a quartz slab on both corners.

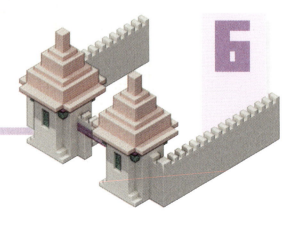

6

7

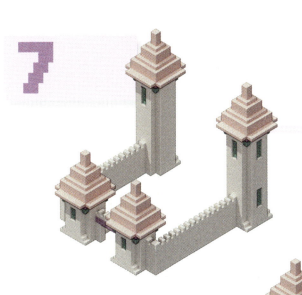

Using the same blocks as before, build two main towers at the back of your palace, with walls 14 blocks tall. Add more prismarine walls for decoration, this time 3 blocks tall.

8

Between your back towers, add a 2-block-tall platform of quartz with purpur blocks in between. Build stairs with quartz slabs coming down into the middle of your palace.

9

Build walls between your back two towers with smooth quartz topped with purpur blocks. Add a 3x3 entranceway, and top with more purpur blocks. Then add four windows filled with light blue stained glass panes.

10 On the top of both walls, build pointed arches with smooth quartz, and fill them in with light blue stained glass windows. Then begin to build the roof with a mixture of cherry planks, stairs and slabs.

11 Continue to build the roof between your walls with the same mixture of blocks, following the shape of your arch as you go up.

12 Finish building your roof so that it meets in the middle, and add 2-block peaks on top.

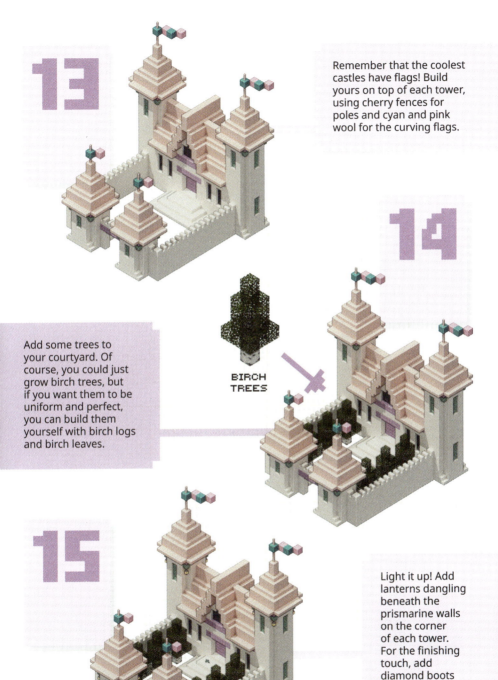

13

Remember that the coolest castles have flags! Build yours on top of each tower, using cherry fences for poles and cyan and pink wool for the curving flags.

14

Add some trees to your courtyard. Of course, you could just grow birch trees, but if you want them to be uniform and perfect, you can build them yourself with birch logs and birch leaves.

BIRCH TREES

15

Light it up! Add lanterns dangling beneath the prismarine walls on the corner of each tower. For the finishing touch, add diamond boots by the stairs!

ATLANTIS ABODE

If you enjoyed living your mermaid life in the lagoon from earlier, you'll sea-riously love this underwater build. Everyone knows that all the coolest mermaids live in Atlantis, so why not make some waves with your very own sunken city beneath the ocean? It'll be fin-tastic!

DIFFICULTY:
★★★☆☆
🕐 35 mins

1

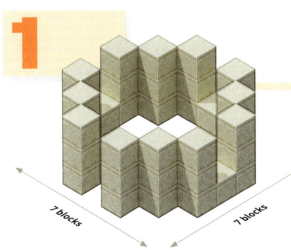

Use cut sandstone to make a circular base for your build, 3 blocks high. On three of the straight sides, leave a 2-block space in the center, and at the front, leave a 3-block space for a door.

7 blocks

7 blocks

2

Add a sandstone slab above the doorway, then fill in the 2-block spaces with sandstone walls. Place sandstone stairs around the corners of your build.

3

Extend your walls up by 4 blocks, adding an indent with sandstone walls at the front, above the door. Then add a layer of cut sandstone on top.

Add another layer of cut sandstone to your walls. Around the outside of the new layer, add some upside-down sandstone stairs. Fill in the center with a mixture of yellow and orange terracotta blocks. Remember to leave a hole in the middle.

FRONT

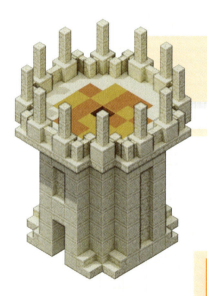

Around the outside, place alternating cut sandstone blocks and sandstone walls. Then add 2 sandstone walls stacked on top of each cut sandstone block.

Place a cut sandstone block on top of each pillar, then connect the spaces between them with upside-down sandstone stairs.

7 On top of the sandstone, add a layer of orange terracotta with a cut sandstone block in the center of each side. Then, mixing in some yellow terracotta, build another layer 1 block in.

Add another layer, 1 block in on just the corners, with yellow terracotta, cut sandstone and a couple of yellow concrete blocks. Finish the dome with a cross of cut sandstone and yellow concrete around it. Place a sea lantern in the middle.

8

9

To make your Atlantis abode look like it's been under the ocean for a while, add a bunch of sea plants, including sea pickles, kelp and sea grass.

91

COMBINATION CHALLENGES

Congratulations! You've completed all the builds in this book. You must be quite the builder. But you're not done yet! Let's see if you're up to a new challenge: combining builds to create new ones.

Listed below are a series of combination challenges. For each of these challenges, we want you to combine the builds using the guides and build tips included in this book. How you combine the builds is completely up to you: You can resize the builds, pick new blocks or improve the design as you see fit.

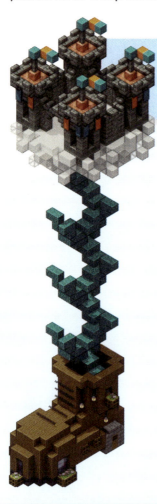

1 BEANSTALK IN A SHOE
If giants live at the top of magical beanstalks, then it makes sense that one of them might drop their shoe!

2 FROG LAGOON
If mermaids aren't your vibe, then perhaps frogs are! Add the frog fountain to this lagoon to make it toad-ally awesome!

3 ATLANTIS MUSHROOM

How cool do these two builds look combined?! And the best part is, the mushroom roof glows, so you'll easily be able to find it underwater.

4 EMERALD LIBRARY

Of course, no emerald city would be complete without an emerald library! Why not combine these two builds?

5 A LIFT TO THE PALACE

Is there a ball going on in the palace? Ride over there in your very own pumpkin carriage!

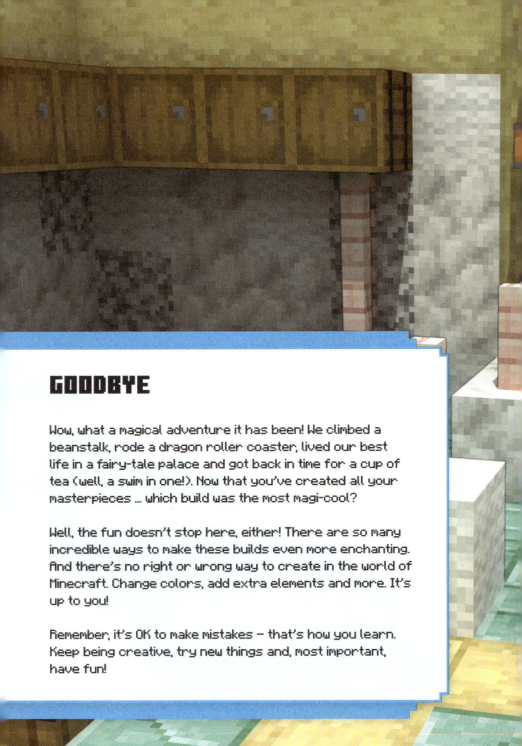

GOODBYE

Wow, what a magical adventure it has been! We climbed a beanstalk, rode a dragon roller coaster, lived our best life in a fairy-tale palace and got back in time for a cup of tea (well, a swim in one!). Now that you've created all your masterpieces ... which build was the most magi-cool?

Well, the fun doesn't stop here, either! There are so many incredible ways to make these builds even more enchanting. And there's no right or wrong way to create in the world of Minecraft. Change colors, add extra elements and more. It's up to you!

Remember, it's OK to make mistakes — that's how you learn. Keep being creative, try new things and, most important, have fun!